ABOUT THE AUTHOR

Owen Burnham was born in a tiny Balanta village called Kouniara in Southern Senegal, West Africa. When only a few days old, he was visited by the famous African healer and diviner Malang Diatta, who bestowed the honour of his name upon him. Owen regularly visits Kouniara, where he is received as a respected member of the community.

Aliou Diatta, Malang's son, is an elder of the village, who has agreed to aid in the writing of this book as the village people are keen that the Balanta culture be more widely known.

With thanks to
Aya and Kae
and their mother
for putting up with me and my dreams

AFRICAN WISDOM

Piatkus Guides

PIATKUS GUIDES

AFRICAN WISDOM

Owen Burnham

PIATKUS

Neither the author nor the publisher is responsible for any harm
caused to anyone undertaking the exercises and meditations in this
book. Anyone who has suffered from a mental or emotional illness
should seek medical advice before attempting the exercises. Some
exercises have been adapted slightly from their traditional African
form in order to make them accessible to a Western readership.

© 2000 Owen Burnham
and Aliou Diatta

First published in 2000 by
Judy Piatkus (Publishers) Ltd
5 Windmill Street
London W1P 1HF
e-mail: info@piatkus.co.uk

For the latest news and information on all our titles, visit
our website at www.piatkus.co.uk

A catalogue record for this book is available from the British Library

ISBN 0-7499-2088-2

Design by Paul Saunders
Edited by Rachel Connolly

Typeset by Action Publishing Technology Ltd., Gloucester
Printed and bound in Great Britain by
Mackays of Chatham PLC

ACKNOWLEDGEMENT

Sincere thanks must go to Aliou Diatta for all his help on this book, since its first beginnings as a mere idea to its final completion. Aliou has been my constant spiritual companion and guide since I was a baby and it was he that imbued in me a sense of wonder at the mysteries and magic all around us in the 'real' world. With the help of Aliou and his wife Rosa Mane, I have been set on a path of discovery. Together both Aliou and Rosa have shown me just what is possible if only we can understand ourselves — and that understanding comes from accepting the spiritual dimensions all around us.

Aliou took me to the sacred forests and sites of the Balanta people and showed me how big the world is, how diverse and how beautiful. There is beauty in everything because, as Aliou says, it all contains the essence of the creator. In the religion and philosophy of Aliou and the

Balanta people there is no aggressive 'marketing' of a certain brand of religion or spirituality. There are only the frameworks of eternal truth which can be found in some form in all the traditional philosophies of the world.

Aliou Diatta is a Balanta, yet his philosophies have echoes all over Africa, from the deepest forests to the sandy deserts. He has a deep wisdom, inherited from countless generations of his ancestors. It is a wisdom that almost defies being put on paper. It is so fluid and so vast, yet Aliou and other elders have a spiritual answer to almost any question whether it concerns the cosmos, where we came from, or other, more earthly, matters. This book can touch only the surface of that body of wisdom.

To Aliou, Rosa and all the Balantas, I am deeply indebted. Without them this book would not have been possible at all.

CONTENTS

INTRODUCTION

'We are born from silence and the forest'
(A Balanta saying)

AFRICAN SPIRITUALITY

I was born in the lush and verdant Casamance region in the south of Senegal, West Africa. Spiritually, the people of Casamance retain many of their old ways and it is in this part of the country that true animists are still found, though sadly, in recent years there has been an increasing erosion of the old religions, due to the influence of both Islam and Christianity, and the increasing rural to urban migration.

I have always had an intense interest in African spiritual life and I believe that this can be traced to the naming ceremony that took place shortly after my birth. On the third day of my life the most respected Balanta spiritual healer, Malang Diatta, arrived with an entourage of women, drummers and followers and in a ceremony marked by dancing and celebration bestowed on me his name, and the greatest honour of my life. I became Kouniara Diatta, Kouniara being the name of the village. The old man studied my face and defined the character and attributes that I would have in later life. He also placed a blessing on me for safety in this life and the next.

The events that took place that day were regarded as unique and extraordinary by the villagers and I was immediately accorded the same status as the local people and given the spiritual and physical freedom to mix with them. I quickly learned to speak Mandinka and Balanta fluently and retain this ability today.

Malang placed me in the care of his eldest son, Aliou Diatta. Under Aliou's guidance I travelled widely and learnt about the spiritual mysteries of Africa. It was a magical and wonderful childhood, during which I learned to walk quietly and absorb the spiritual energy that surrounds us. From the earliest times, Aliou took me into the sacred forests, taught me how to sense the spirits in nature, let me witness the ceremonies at sacred trees and rocks, and imbued in me a sense of poetry and wonder which I retain still. Aliou and I retain the strong bond that was formed all those years ago; we meet often and he continues to teach me.

When I was eighteen years old, I moved to England, completed a degree and learned a different way of life, yet

Africa is in me and my spirit is always in Africa. I return frequently, often for extended periods.

Aliou is an old man now. His journey, that has been mine as well for so long, will soon be at an end, yet even in these circumstances he teaches me wisdom, acceptance, and the value of all life, both in the present and the future. He is not afraid of death, seeing it only as a temporary barrier between the visible and invisible. Aliou's life revolves around his nine children and wife Rosa. He and Rosa regularly make long journeys into the forest where Aliou will contact other Balantas for sacred ceremonies and for 'learning'. Being such a humble man, he is the first to say that he is still learning; I wonder where that leaves me ...

Aliou's religion is called 'Boisee', a complicated set of beliefs revolving around energy forces in the earth and other natural objects. Nature spirits are everywhere and each must be respected in a certain way; adherence to tradition is all important. Aliou has been, and still is, my gateway into the African spiritual world. He has extensive contacts among, and knowledge of, African peoples and their beliefs, and is especially knowledgeable about the Mandinka, Manjack, Mankanye, Diola, Birassou, Papel and Wolof people. He understands that the old ways are fast vanishing, at least in a pure form, and is keen that they be preserved. He is truly a magical man, and without him this book could not have been written.

THE CREATION

The spirituality found within Africa dates back to ancient times, and throughout this book you will find references to the creation of the world, primarily in relation to the Mandinka people who inhabit much of West Africa. Theirs is a complicated creation story, full of beauty and symbolism, which is similar in some ways to the beliefs of surrounding peoples such as the Balanta.

The original creator, *Gla* (meaning emptiness), created the universe through a succession of spirals and circular movements which gave rise to vibrations and life over a great length of time. It is a story that is often linked with present-day practices, such as the reverence attached to eggs by traditional peoples who believe we are in the 'egg of the world' created by God (*Gla* created God when giving consciousness to the universe). The spirals of the creation are often still present in the magic drawings that appear on sacred wooden altars or stones, and for the Balantas, Manjacks, Mankanyes and others, the eternal circle of life, 'Kara', is remembered in many of their magical ceremonies and reflected in the widespread use of standing stones placed in circles or small wooden stakes placed around trees or in sacred parts of the house. The African people see the results of their creation daily and indeed believe that creative processes are still being carried out on a daily basis. It is a vibrant belief, an almost unshakeable faith and one I hope to transmit through the pages of this book.

African people are intensely spiritual and have an inner belief in God. God is often viewed as an artist who moulded humans from dust after the creation of the world and universe. All African peoples attach an importance to God but often see the creator as far removed from humans, in the same way that we are far removed from insects such as ants. God uses emissaries to connect with us. To the Balanta people these are the Aboule spirits, which appear in the form of egg-shaped electric blue lights that are truly astonishingly beautiful and moving. The spirit of God is in all things, however, and provides the rain and sun that humanity needs for survival.

Growing up in a remote and small African village gave me a unique perspective on the traditions and wisdom of the local people. There is a spirituality in everything, termed the 'ni' by Mandinka people and 'ki' by the Balantas. In fact it is safe to say that there are few moments in life or death that are not touched spiritually; life is a drama, played out against the background of the earth, sky, forest, trees and, of course, the ever-present spirit world. This spirit world is both a part of the creative 'ni', as well as emanating from it.

AFRICAN WISDOM

From this spirituality spring individual aspects of N'gala (God) and its wisdom. There are many 'wisdoms' in Africa, and indeed, many wise people. Wisdom and advice-giving are an expected prerequisite for old age and take many forms, but again all are recognised as emanating from the 'ni' which itself came from *Gla*. There is a wisdom in *all* things, which humans should note and learn from. In addition, there are certain specialists (*Jambacosso*) in each society who have special powers of communication with the animals and plants. The knowledge they gain can be converted into advice which is given out to villagers and people who may need help, after cutting down the wrong tree, for example. The tree spirit in question will be angry and may cause problems for the person who did the cutting. Through intercession the *Jambacosso* may be able to divert problems before they can happen, though this could be at some small (usually symbolic) cost to the person in trouble.

While this may sound dangerously complicated, it provides an important message which has largely been forgotten in the Western world; that unless nature and its resources are protected and used sensibly the earth/mother nature will take revenge eventually. It is a message from the heart of a people that still believe in a greater neutral power that can be both benign, beautiful and savage. I hope that through this book *we* will be able to show the beauty and fragility of the world in which we live.

For rural Africans life is both a struggle and a joy. In many ways their existence is hard and unrelenting, but they remain a happy people filled with music, rhythm and dance which is spontaneous and emerges from the heart.

My most tangible memories are of evenings spent in the company of a fire, gently talking people and the buzzing hum of the mysterious *kambalaon* harp. At such times a storyteller will usually emerge from the flickering firelight and shadows and begin to talk, of life, the stars, the past, and the future. At times he will say a prayer to one of his ancestors in such a pure, clear way that it is almost poetry, spoken with feeling and passion and the deepest love. This is the Africa I am privileged to have grown up in, with its mixture of emotions, smells, sounds and dreams.

In the pages that follow I will take you through the spiritual world of the Balanta people, a subjective world which relies on utter trust and belief in the supernatural. Through the rituals described it is possible to dispel the fear that is so often present in people living in developed countries who have little or no experience of the supernatural world. Instead of this uncertainty and fear I would like to show how it is possible to reacquaint yourself with the unseen world. By following some of the exercises in this book it is possible to get back in touch with spiritual pathways that you may have been unaware of, and through this you may develop skills that would otherwise have remained hidden. Above all else, this book is an attempt to help you find yourself, and, ultimately, fulfilment.

1

PAN-AFRICAN WISDOMS

Sub-Saharan Africa is a vast area encompassing a wide range of cultures which span habitats ranging from true desert to dense forest and huge swamps. However, despite the differences in language and culture that exist all over the continent, certain common themes run through traditional African societies from Senegal in the north of West Africa, to the Republic of South Africa at the southern tip of the continent. In each of these environments, humans have evolved both culturally *and* spiritually. This physical and spiritual adaptation makes Africa a truly remarkable and unique place.

THE CREATOR

A traditional African belief is in a nebulous creator, an idea of 'God' that is far removed from the Western one.

The African creator emerged from nothing. It is neither male nor female but rather a force throughout the universe. To the Mandinka-speaking people of Mali and Senegal this is the concept of *'mana'*, the divine power which is manifested in all things living and inanimate. It is *mana* that holds all things together and has done so since the earliest points of creation. *Mana* helped blend all the creative elements in a whirlwind and then held them there until the process could be accomplished fully. The creation forms a link with present-day beliefs in African societies, even if these are abstract.

It is important to note that in African thought the creator is *distant*, unconcerned with the affairs of mankind, except indirectly via animal and spirit emissaries.

The Aboule

Between the creator and humans are several types of spiritual being. Firstly, there are the Aboule, which the Balanta people of Guinea Bissau and Casamance believe were designed to help in the creation of the universe. They were each sent out with one of the vibrations of creation so whatever they touched was given some of the life force of the creator. The Aboule exist all around us and are helpful to humans though they continue to carry out their creative duties.

The Foiro

Secondly, there are the Foiro spirits which exist in the neutral state and must be appeased at certain places, for example at the crossroads of two paths where prayers and offerings are made. The Foiro emerged as a result of mistakes made during the creation, which led to less than perfect beings. In an angry state, the Foiro can cause misery and mischief to humans, and are believed to do so all over Africa. The Foiro spirits are said to inhabit the distant parts of the third layer of sky. It is a complicated idea, but to traditional people in Africa, there is a belief in seven skies, each with their own entities and character (*see* Chapter 6).

ANCESTOR SPIRITS

In addition to these two spiritual levels, there exist the spirits of the ancestors, as well as those of animals, plants and the earth. Ancestor spirits are the most important and are all around us, though they live in their own dimensions of time and only come into our world when they choose to. They are generally widely respected in Africa. This is not always the case however, and sometimes fear of the ancestors replaces respect, for example, among the Lango people of Uganda. The ancestor spirits remain around the living and act as intermediaries between them and the rest of the spirit world. However, since ancestor spirits exist in a world between death and rebirth they must be reborn with help from the living. This creates a *symbiotic* relationship between humans and their ancestors; they are eventually reborn into human society only if humans remember them and make regular offerings of food and prayers. In return, the ancestor or shadow of the deceased will help its living relatives.

It is normal for ancestral spirits to appear to living family members, and the first appearance is normally made towards a child either in a dream or during the waking state. On such an occasion the child is expected to report the appearance. Once the incident has been reported, the adults of the family must try to make contact. This process is carried out with deep respect and ritual since at all times the ancestor must feel it is being honoured. If angered, its rebirth into the human world may be delayed or prevented.

Contacting the Ancestor Spirits

Since only certain people can communicate with the ancestor easily, one of these must be contacted and the situation explained. In Mandinka, these people 'with the greatest wisdom' are known as *kunfao*, which literally means that their 'heads are full of spiritual abilities'. The *kunfao* or equivalent arranges a meeting time, usually in the family home of the ancestor. Offerings of food and wine are made at the door of the house and the ancestor is asked to enter. The *kunfao* may then play an ancestral tune on a special harp, flute or drum which is believed to call the spirit. In most cases the spirit will manifest itself. It may be only the *kunfao* that can see it, but if the character of the spirit were strong in life, it may be able to make itself visible to all. In some cases it may manifest itself as a voice which emerges spontaneously from a sacred object such as the horn of a roan antelope or an earthenware pot. When the ancestor spirit appears physically it takes the form of 'shifting smoke' and the *kunfao* can then question the apparition on the family's behalf. The quavering, accentless voice of an ancestral spirit is instantly recognisable and very strange.

The first time I witnessed one of these ceremonies, Aliou and I were in a small village near Kouniara. It was remote and simple with houses arranged in the circle so characteristic of Balanta people. During our day-long walk through the forest to the village, we made several stops at sacred sites where we made offerings to the spirits. At another place we lit a fire and burned some fragrant bark from a special tree we encountered. The various rituals we carried out created a fantastic atmosphere, where the light and shadows from the forest blended in a spectacular way and seemed to mingle with the smell of the bark. In addition, our 'smoke bath' had impregnated us with the mysterious smell of the bark which Aliou explained was pleasant to his ancestors.

Before we reached the village we stopped at the edge of a forest pool where we dug some yellow clay which we painted on our faces. We also obtained some reddish pigment from a crushed termite hill and added this to the yellow. Then, in a circle of water, Aliou lit a small fire and roasted the rest of the bark, noting carefully how the flames went down at the end and the pattern of the ashes they left. From these he deduced that we should enter the village from the west side where we should again make a small offering. We then took the ashes and added them to the red and yellow pigments. The pigments represented the ancestral colours of the chief whose spirit was to be contacted, while the ashes linked us to the ancestral spirits of Aliou.

It must have been a strange sight for the villagers when we arrived. Here I was, a white man, speaking fluent Mandinka yet painted in the colours of the ancestors and mourning. While people tried to absorb this image that was both real and impossible at the same time, they saw the diminutive figure of the great herbalist and diviner, Aliou Diatta, small of stature but a spiritual giant. Any uncertainty the people had regarding me was quickly dispelled and we were swept toward the current chief's house where formal greetings followed and I passed out the mandatory red and white cola nuts to several of the village elders. They knew of me and talked interestedly among themselves about my naming ceremony. We were instructed to follow an old woman who quickly led us through the dusty village streets towards a mud house with a small green mango tree outside. Children quickly appeared with stools and we were instructed to wait for the *Jambacosso*, a certain Soloba, the most famous medium in the area, named after the big leopards that communicated with him in dreams.

Dusk was falling when he made his arrival, accompanied by one drummer who fell silent as he approached us. We rose and greeted the great man. Without much formality or delay the medium sprinkled water and milk in front of the door and announced his presence loudly three times. The inside of the round house was dark and cool. A small fire was quickly lit in the centre of the room and by the light of this I could see a few possessions that had belonged to Idrissa, the deceased who Soloba would shortly contact. Soloba laid out a mat on the floor and from his bag produced a series of magical substances including lions' claws and cowrie shells. He hung a large roan antelope horn from a nail in the wall and then burned some leaves that produced a strange sweet smell. By now only a female relative, Mariama, the sister of the deceased, remained with us and the door was shut. The atmosphere was vibrant with expectation. A thin white, fragrant smell rose in the spirals of smoke from the fire as the medium closed his eyes and began to rock gently, whispering in a voice that rose and fell. He then produced a small three-holed bamboo flute and began to play the haunting notes that will echo in my mind forever.

Suddenly Soloba began to talk quickly to something unseen that had entered the room. He stood up, beads of sweat on his face and looked intently into the shadows, asking questions. It seemed that the spirit had been troubling living family members, especially Mariama. Having asked the questions the medium sat down. Then a strange quavering voice emerged from the darkness. It was eerie, flat and toneless with no accent. The voice spoke in Mandinka and began answering the questions. By this time the medium was staring wide-eyed in the direction of the horn. He later told me that the spirit had emerged from the horn and stood beside it during our meeting. From time to time Soloba produced his flute and played again.

This incredible experience lasted about an hour, during which time we were glued to the unfolding story of why the spirit of this man had felt it had to return. For myself, it was an incredible and enlightening experience. I would later participate in other 'questioning' ceremonies, but this one in particular will always remain with me. The flat, toneless voice of the spirit and the honesty of the medium made trickery an impossibility. Indeed, at the end, Soloba looked exhausted, having dispensed so much spiritual energy during the meeting. Mariama followed the instructions given to her by the spirit and she has had no more problems since.

The Advice of the Ancestor Spirits

The reasons behind ancestral visits are varied. In many parts of Africa ancestors maintain a contact with the living in order to warn them of forthcoming situations. Aliou Diatta, for example, regularly enters into dream communications with his ancestors who appear in order to advise him before he makes any major decisions or long journeys. In these situations, the ancestors will advise on the route to take, and will notify of any dangers on the way. To the really skilled *kunfao* like Aliou, it is possible to enter into dream communication with the ancestral spirits at will. In these circumstances, more than just advice is given; Aliou may be given news from the world of the spirits and messages to pass on to living family members.

The ancestors may also advise on issues such as an inability to become pregnant. In this case, the ancestral spirit may instruct that certain rituals be carried out to achieve the desired goal. One such ritual involves the use of water; as it is often said, 'water is the creator' and moulder of life. Before sleeping, a calabash of water is taken from a nearby source such as a deep well or mountain stream. Purity is essential. Beside the calabash or bowl is laid a stick or branch of the ancestral tree, along with some fresh leaves from the same plant. These are bound together and placed next to the bed of the person that wishes to conceive. It is believed that the creative spirit will move and mould the child in the womb using water. The prayer placed on the leaves and water asks that the creative spirit will make a child 'as young and fresh as the green leaves' that are placed with the moulding stick. It is also prayed that the child that is born will have the attributes of the ancestral tree, including sturdiness and long life. The water is stirred seven times with the stick and a single leaf is taken from the cluster and placed in the bowl. This is followed by the prayer: 'May life emerge from the swirling that is beyond our knowledge or even our dreams, and then may stillness descend and a perfect child be born.' Normally the prayer is answered in an uncannily perfect way.

Sacred Sites

Ancestor spirits traditionally live near the village they inhabited as humans. They especially frequent trees such as the Baobab and Kapok, one of which is often the sacred tree of the village with a clearing kept around it.

Such sacred sites are treated with great reverence, and stones or pieces of wood are left in certain positions to represent the ancestors. However, small caves and strange rock formations, especially where water is present, are also regarded as important to the spirits.

The Mashona people of southern Africa go to such places to collectively enquire of the ancestral spirits. By the ceremonial pouring of sacred water, the site is purified for human usage. The Mashona equivalent of the West African *kunfao* then enters the purified site and begins a communion with the village ancestors who are believed to inhabit sacred rocks and waters, much as in the Balanta culture.

The spirituality of rocks, water and fire is another important theme in African thought. Small sacred stones may be placed in circles near to a small fire to represent the universe, the ancestors and the continuity between the past and present phases of creation. Stones are said to be the resting place of the Foiro spirits, which hide among these in order to spy on passers-by. It is wise to offer eggs or libations of wine when passing such places and to ask for safety on your journey. Water is the source of all life and is usually the abode of spirits. Rivers, lakes and streams are often believed to be the homes of water sprites and spirits, which must be respected before entering or crossing the water. If disrespect is shown, these entities may grab a person's shadow and pull them into the river and drown them.

THE MULTI-DIMENSIONAL WORLD

The world of the traditional African person is one of mystery, danger and the link between the seen and unseen. It is also a world of continuity, from the past to the present, and this is most easily seen in the trees, rocks and great natural wonders that are all around. It is a world in which wisdom and knowledge are the keys to survival in the multi-dimensional spiritual universe where we are never far from the past, present and future as represented by the ancestral spirits that are all around us. In so many ways we are influenced by them and often fall prey to their wishes without knowing it. For this reason it is extremely important to be aware of the intricate yet often unrealised world around us. Through the *kunfao* we are afforded a glimpse of our ancestors, the numerous Foiro spirits as well as the spirits of trees and the earth. There are entities of light, others that give off darkness, some with many eyes and teeth, and yet others that 'see by thinking' alone. To many people it may seem a terrifying and somewhat improbable world, but to the traditional people I have been honoured to learn from, 'everything is possible', both in life and in dreams. To the Balanta, Mankanye, Bichog, Malinke, Senufo and others these entities are ever present and we as humans survive by respecting and understanding them.

One thing I have learned is that no matter how terrifying or obnoxious the entities may be, they do tend to be neutral and are capable of choices both good and bad. They also usually enter into a relationship with humans for their own reasons. Just as we cannot fully enter the spirit world, so they cannot fully enter ours and require help from humans to carry out certain tasks in our plane. However, being spiritually separate, even the most innocent of encounters can cause us humans great alarm and this can cause fear and misunderstanding on *both* sides. Spirits who are rejected through fear may become angered and cause great harm to humans. With this in mind, an understanding has built up between humans and the spirit world whereby spirits often begin communicating with adults (whose fear is greatest) through children, who often have no fear of the spirit world at all.

DREAMING

Ancestral spirits are everywhere and may make their presence known through illness, depression or a feeling of unease that never seems to go away. They also often appear in dreams, though people living in developed countries usually dismiss dreams as the random workings of the brain during sleep. The first thing I will say in relation to this is: *pay attention to your dreams, they are important. They are a channel for the spirit world.* Dreams are the means by which the invisible can become visible. If you regularly see a person in your dreams, listen to what they say. Do not dismiss it, especially if the dream is clear and lucid, and always follow the instructions you are given.

In the case of an illness or depression that appears to have no medical cause, be especially vigilant; there is likely to be a spiritual cause, and finding it is not as hard as it may seem.

EXERCISE

Ni Mala (Lighting the Soul)

The ancestors are attracted to fire, water, and milk.

♦ Find a place in your home, such as a table, and before going to bed spread a cloth on the table of the colour preferred by the ancestral spirit, if you think you know who that spirit is. If you are not sure who is trying to make contact then choose a blue cloth; a blue like cobalt is a good colour.

♦ Also on the table place a small floating candle in a bowl of clean water (in Africa a fire would be lit). Next to it place another bowl of water and next to that a small bowl of milk. The candle flame represents the purity of eternity, the fiery first wind that helped in the creation. It is an eternal link between humanity and the creator. The bowl of water represents life, both now and in the future. It is never ending and since it is said by Africans that 'water never loses its way', so the spirit will succeed in its journey to fulfilment and rebirth. The bowl of milk is a representation of the ultimate purity of your request. It indicates sincerity in all things pertaining to the ancestral spirit. Never use milk if you are not totally sure of your own feelings. If you think you know who the ancestor is then you could also use a food that they adored in life. This is a symbol to show the ancestral spirit that you are concerned for them and that you are ready for them to reach you.

♦ Dedicate the table to the spirit and ask that it will appear. This can be done to a background of atmospheric music, either of your own choice or the music preferred by the person in life.

♦ Imagine that you are surrounding the table in light of the purest kind. Close your eyes and concentrate on the questions you wish to be answered. Concentrate on the person you wish to contact you. Imagine every detail, recall everything you can, and know that they will be near you even as you are doing it. They will find as much comfort in the ritual as you do.

- After this (it can take as long as you choose), leave the table and go to bed.

- While sleeping you may dream, and in that state you will be able to find out who the spirit is and why they have been trying to make contact. Follow any instructions carefully. Remember we are in a symbiotic relationship. Our ancestral spirits need our help and can intercede for us among higher spirits that may ultimately hold our destinies in their power. Do not be afraid. A spirit will not want to frighten you and if you have fear of any sort it will not want to aggravate that.

I believe that this simple ceremony can put people back in touch with their past. I have seen variations of it played out in African homes and it is often very effective; but remember that the spirits will only come if they want to, if they need help or if they feel they can help you.

2

THE WISDOM OF ANIMALS

'Animals are mysterious to people, but less so than plants are,' an old African woman once told me. She was the guardian of a sacred site in the Bandar forest, where some elders of the Balanta community had invited me for 'teaching'. This old woman was totally at ease with herself and the world, for though she lacked a formal Western-style education, she had her own education and belief system, and was completely sustained by a multi-dimensional world of plant, human and animal spirits. I was immediately struck, on this occasion as on so many others, by the sincerity and ease with which the old woman performed the simple ceremonies that had sustained her and her people for countless generations. There was wisdom in the simplicity and a total acceptance of the reasons for and results of the rituals.

Rituals and ceremonies are an everyday part of life for animistic people all over Africa. They help them to survive in a world populated by beings that remain neutral towards humans only when placated with offerings and prayers. It is a world far removed from that known by most people in developed countries, but to Africans our lives and those of the spirits all around us are closely entwined, though ultimately separate. It is through understanding what is happening around us that we can learn to harness the spiritual elements in all objects, both inanimate and animate. The world of animal spirits is especially close to that of humans and there is often a strong belief in the interchangeability of human and animal souls both during life and after death. In this chapter I will attempt to explain some of the mysteries and wisdoms that are inherent in the world of animals.

ANIMAL SPIRITS

Animals are distinct and different from humans. However, in traditional African thought it is ourselves who changed at a point in the creative process when evil entered the world through human actions. Animals remained as they always had been, while humans were punished by separation from the other worlds, and since that time humanity has had to learn a way back in. When humans and animals separated animals retained the ability to see into the spiritual realm while we largely lost that ability. This aspect of the animal soul has been widely exploited by traditional African societies, who contact animal spirits to act as intermediaries during divination when the help of the ancestral (human) spirits is required. Animal spirits are in effect a link between the present and the past.

An example of this is found among the Niomingke people of Senegal in West Africa. Certain initiated members of the community have the ability to contact the spirits of hyenas, since these great carnivores are believed to be able to 'see into the world of the ancestors'. For the Niomingke, the hyena is quite simply a semi-divine animal that is never harmed, since to harm one of these creatures would be tantamount to harming an ancestor or even another villager. The transfer of souls between a human and a hyena is widespread and similar beliefs are found all over Africa, though using other highly respected animals, including leopards, cats, giant snakes and lizards.

It is believed by the Papel people of Guinea Bissau that they can transform themselves into many animals, including pythons and leopards. In this case, the transfer is believed to be a literal one and is achieved through a deep knowledge and understanding of the animal spirit involved.

Whatever an educated Western person may believe, they must always remember to keep an open mind when dealing with African spiritual matters and to remember that 'all things are possible in the spirit world', as I have been told on several occasions when talking to African elders about spiritual matters that on the surface seem to defy logic and rational thinking. To the people carrying out the practices described there is utter belief and a deep conviction that the expected results *will* occur, and this I feel is the key to understanding the wisdom of animals in greater depth.

The Animal/Human Relationship

Animal spirits are regarded as being similar to those of humans, although humans are never reincarnated as animals. Each type of creature has its own specific spiritual code similar to the genetic code employed by scientists. In the early period of creation, each animate and inanimate object was given its own 'vibration' which gives it its character to this day. To humans and other animals was also given the seed of consciousness itself. So from the start, humans and animals existed together; neither ate the other, relying instead on food that fell in balls from heaven. This was a time of *universal spirituality*, with animals and humans being able to communicate with each other easily, 'since our languages were not separate then' (Aliou Diatta).

It was at this time that certain animal/human links were

forged which have managed to survive until the present day, for example the special link between the aardvark and the Balanta Kanja people, and between the manatee (sea cow) and the Fulani people, from whom it is said the first manatee came when a Fulani woman fell into the magic river and was transformed into one of the great creatures. As I have mentioned, the Niomingke believe that hyenas and humans have a special link, while the Kubunka people of Guinea Bissau believe that the giant forest eagle carries away the souls of the dead.

After evil entered the world via the human character, the nature of the human/animal relationship changed in general terms. Humans were punished when they began to eat other animals, so introducing death into the world. Some animals did remain sacred, but only the Shamans of the Americas and Asia and the *Jambacosso* and *Foura Tiyo* of Africa retained the knowledge of how to contact them. It is these people who truly understand the wisdom of animals, with all its depth and profound beauty.

The Totem Animal

Animal spirits wander between the worlds of humans and the creator. They exist in a variety of forms and can even take a human shape. They are believed to inhabit our world but also to have access to a spiritual world that is full of nebulous shapes and sounds. Where a human family has a relationship with an animal spirit, the animal is adopted as a totem of the family. A symbiotic relationship is thus formed where the animal spirit provides help and advice to the family; usually through appearances in dreams or by means of unusual behaviour. The totem animal must never be harmed, and it must be respected and offered food and palm wine at specific times each day.

I well remember a situation when an ancestral totem animal was offended. I was staying with a Balanta family in the village of Kolda in central Casamance, in the south of Senegal. It was a beautiful setting on the edge of the town and we enjoyed many fine conversations together in the evenings, during which time the distant grunt of hyenas would cause Dabo Mane, the elder of the house, to put more wood on the fire. We woke up one morning and I noticed a small gathering around Dabo's small daughter, Fatou. I approached and saw that her eyes were tightly shut; they could not even be prized open. Her worried mother, Isatou, strapped her on her back, and amid shouts of good luck and encouragement set off towards the Catholic Mission station where the nuns had a dispensary. When they arrived the nuns were concerned. The child's eyes were not leaking pus or in any way damaged. They just would not open. They told the mother that she would have to go 400 kilometres to the main hospital and maybe there they would be able to help. Isatou returned home and after discussions with Dabo and other family members they decided that an old diviner called Bouba should be consulted. I went with Isatou to see Bouba and found him to be a man of exceptional spiritual power. He took the child in his arms and stared intently into her face. Two flies buzzed around her and he chased them away. After a few minutes he gave Fatou back to her mother and produced some cowrie shells. Using only seven of these he began to divine.

In his small, quiet room the young girl's destiny was decided. The 'pale shells' told him that Fatou had been caught by the family's ancestral totem animal, the river soft-shell turtle. It transpired that Isatou had neglected to go to the river and throw food into the water at the usual time when she should have invoked the spirit. The old diviner told her that she should go immediately and throw cola nuts, couscous (millet variety) and milk into the river at Kolda. At the same time she should ask forgiveness of the turtle spirit.

Together we followed the path down to the river, carrying Fatou. We bought the food items on the way. The river was dark and menacing as we reached the bank and I shivered involuntarily. As our eyes adjusted to the darkness I was able to make out the glimmer of stars in the dark water. Fatou began to cry. I watched Isatou prepare the offering, and then slowly and respectfully she began to throw food into the river, speaking to the water spirit at the same time: 'I, Isatou, ask your forgiveness for my neglect and irresponsible behaviour. I was busy and I neglected you. Now you have closed the eyes of my daughter. I ask your forgiveness and beg you to allow my daughter to have her sight back. Let her eyes open. I offer you these cola nuts, red and white, and this couscous and milk. Take my humble offering and let my child be free. Thank you.' Her heartfelt words entered the innumerable sounds of the universe and suddenly something moved in the water. Small waves lapped at our feet and I shivered again. I looked at Fatou and to my utter amazement her eyes were open and she was gazing around wide-eyed and smiling. It was a truly wonderful moment and I understood then why and how the wisdom of animals is widely acknowledged in Africa, and how it may be harnessed through trances, dreams or by meditation. As an old Kabunka man once told me: 'If we imagine, we become ...', however this profound thought simplifies the deep spiritual significance and knowledge inherent in understanding animal wisdom and magic.

Contacting an Animal Spirit

It is not as impossible or difficult as it may seem to contact an animal spirit. It is achieved through a deeper awareness of oneself and of the spiritual world. It is in *feeling* that we acquire the knowledge necessary to reach out into other worlds and into ourselves. In most cases we have an animal spirit associated with us already though we may not be aware of this; *awareness* is the key to knowledge. An animal spirit will normally make itself known to someone it wishes to help in this life. Dreams containing the animal, especially if they are often repeated, are a common sign that an attempt at contact is being made.

My own animal is the dwarf crocodile (*Couto*) that is famous for living on dry land and for being tame and inoffensive. Scientists who have studied these tiny crocodiles often speak of them as being of a shy and elusive nature. They also associate them more with the water than the dry land, again the opposite of my experience. To myself and the Balanta people, these crocodiles are emissaries of goodwill from the creator or the Aboule; to see one is extremely good luck. Crocodiles may appear in dreams or be contacted personally. Certain wise people even believe that they can enter the soul of the dwarf crocodile to learn its wisdoms.

I remember the first time I was taken to 'meet' a dwarf crocodile. I walked with an elder through the fringing forests along a narrow path with rice fields on one side and patches of forest with palms on the other. It was the middle of the day, a time when scientific thought suggested that dwarf crocodiles would be in the water. We left the path and walked towards a clump of palms and other trees isolated in the dry savannah. The elder stopped about a hundred metres from the clump of trees and gently whistled a three-syllable note. After a slight pause we moved on. We reached the trees and my elder pointed to a burrow beneath some roots. It was wide with a smooth, well worn entrance. Again the elder whistled gently. We walked around the clump of trees and on our return were rewarded by the appearance of a dwarf crocodile laying in its burrow. As we watched from two metres away it emerged fully and gazed at us intently with its dark eyes.

I watched quietly and in awe as the elder closed his eyes and began whispering his thoughts to the creature. It appeared as mesmerised as him. For about fifteen minutes this strange meeting continued before the small crocodile slowly lowered its head and retreated backwards into its tunnel. The elder explained to me that the dwarf crocodile represented a link with one of his ancestors since the crocodile had been his totem animal in life. The communication appeared totally genuine as things that the elder was 'told' later came true in my presence. I have since been to other such meetings and have never failed to be deeply impressed by what I have seen and felt.

Spontaneous thought is another means via which animals can enter into communication with humans. In these situations the same animal reoccurs in thoughts at any time and for no reason. In a dream, for example, a leopard may appear on successive nights or over a period of time. It will look at the dreamer in a certain way; the look is almost human, but as Soloba Sajio once said to me 'there is a difference in the eyes'. If the dreams are ignored, the leopard may appear physically to the person and then all doubts are cast aside, 'for the eyes of a leopard in dreams are far less intense than those of a totem leopard in life'. If this sounds far-fetched then remember that awareness and acceptance are the keys to understanding this wisdom. Without acceptance and belief a dream is just a dream and a whole world of animal wisdom is untapped.

EXERCISE

Ni Kiloh (The Soul Calling)

♦ Once the animal has made contact it is important to go to a quiet spot; a wood is ideal. As you walk through the wood, use your intuition to choose a tree. Choose the first tree that strikes you as being strange, different or in any way notable. Do not dwell on why this tree is being chosen and not another. As the Mankanye people say 'the tree chooses the person'.

♦ Once the tree has been chosen, find eight small stones, about golf ball size.

♦ Clear a space in front of the tree so that the earth is exposed. On this cleared patch place seven stones in a circle big enough for a person to sit in. Put the last stone in the middle of the circle.

♦ Between the centre stone and the outer ring place two small pebbles (one on each side of the centre stone). These represent yourself and the animal spirit.

♦ The site must then be initiated and this will require a small amount of milk, the symbol of purity, water, the symbol of life, and alcohol, the drink of the creator. Pour a libation of alcohol among the roots of the tree, just in front of the circle (not in it). Then take some water and pour it in a ring around the stones.

♦ If you are a woman you must step over this four times, since this is the female symbol in creation. A man should step over it three times. While doing this, ask the animal spirit to make itself known as soon as possible.

♦ Then take a little of the milk and pour it over the centre stone, again, whispering the request. Normally the answer will become apparent very quickly, usually through a dream when the animal will talk to you, or through deep convictions of thought that appear to come from nowhere.

Domestic Animals

If you feel that one of your domestic animals, a cat or dog for example, is attempting to contact you, it is possible to take this further via a simple ritual in which anyone can participate.

EXERCISE

Kurungo Landi (Placing the Shells)

◆ Take twenty-three cowrie shells (these are often sold in art and craft shops). These represent the twenty-two spirals of thought in creation, plus yourself. Place the twenty-two in a circle and place the last one in the top half of the circle on a piece of coloured cloth laid out on the floor. This should be your own spiritual colour, usually your favourite colour in everyday life.

◆ Take a small bunch of hairs from the animal in question and place them in the circle below the middle shell. Close your eyes and think only of the questions you want to ask. Be honest. There should be nothing frivolous in this. Never attempt to contact any spirit without good reason as this can be dangerous.

◆ Transfer your thoughts onto the hair and the middle cowrie which represents yourself. Link the two in your mind.

◆ Gently put a drop of milk on the hairs and the middle shell and using the same intense thought processes as previously, ask the animal spirit for its help and for confirmation that the spirit you are attempting to contact is indeed the one that you sought. Take as long as you want. Again do not be frivolous. It may turn out that you have a *different* animal spirit.

I must warn against trying to contact a pet because it is cute or cuddly. These are not valid reasons for contacting a spirit and in such circumstances nothing will happen (at best), or the animal may appear in a dream and state in no uncertain terms that a mistake was made. This can be frightening. Animals in dreams may look the same as in real life, except that they are larger and have a different look in their eyes. Their communication with us is by thought.

When an animal appears following successful participation in the above ritual you will know immediately. Always remember to keep your promises and do as it says in return for the advice it will give. In time the animal may begin to appear regularly in your thoughts and dreams, and you may even see it when you are not expecting it. For example, you may have left your dog or cat at home and gone out when suddenly you see your pet in the street looking at you. It will then disappear. The appearance is only for you and is not sinister. Carry out the ritual when you get home to find out what is happening. It may be an important message.

After each ritual you should rinse the hairs and place them in a small sealed container, an earthenware jar is best. These hairs contain some of the elements of the animal's soul and are very important since they are the first hairs you used in making contact. Keep them safe always. Keep the cowrie shells safe elsewhere, in a leather pouch if you have one. Always thank them as you put them away. They contain magical properties once you have used them and should be treated with the greatest respect. You will get your answers in dreams. Pay attention to them at all times.

The Sacred Site

The stones you have set up must always be treated with reverence and respect. They represent the universe, the egg of the world in creation. The creator is represented by the stone in the middle around which everything revolves. The initiated site is now sacred. It is a link between the universe, the earth, the trees and ourselves and animals. It is the key into a world of greater wisdom and must always be looked after and carefully maintained; always respect it as a living entity. If the site is not maintained for some time it is important to provide an explanation and apology during the next visit. Food should be dedicated to the site at each visit. *Never* eat at the site without leaving a small amount for the stones, usually in the tree roots. Always eat the same food that has been offered to the stones, and eat in the presence of the stones. Since this is a living site it will provide answers to questions and these will be quite clear.

The animal spirit can be contacted at times when decisions are hard to make for some reason. In times of illness or unease, the thought or dream response will guide you towards certain plant cures or will indicate that certain small ceremonies must be carried out. If the advice is followed the situation will improve rapidly.

Animal wisdom is the wisdom of eternal rebirth, and the movement of the stars. It is also the wisdom of the creative spirit that still moves through the quiet places of the earth creating beauty and rejuvenation. It is a wisdom that provides our minds with clarity and simplicity, and once we have freed our minds from the barriers that modern societies create then our thoughts and feelings are free to be intuitive and we can find our own spirituality linked to that of the universe. This is the wisdom of animals. It is eternal and waiting to be grasped.

Slow breathing and meditation can also be practised in the presence of the stones and this will clarify the mind and thoughts. Knowledge becomes immediately available, the solutions to insurmountable problems become clear. It is a way of rejoining our spirits to those of the trees, the earth, the soil, our dreams and the silence. If we achieve inner silence we are close to the creator.

I hope that the rituals mentioned will enable a clearer understanding of who and what we are. It is a learning process. Do not expect everything at once but learn and advance slowly. Be prepared to ask questions, and be especially prepared for the answers. Serious questions will be answered with serious answers. Remember you are playing by the rules of the spiritual world rather than your own. Be good and kind and the spirits will be as well. These are some of the wisdoms of animals. With belief and perseverance they can take you into a deeper sense of peace and tranquillity.

3

THE WISDOM OF PLANTS

Plants exist in their own special silence which is closer to that of the original creation than for any other life form. It is also said of plants that they 'emanated directly from the thoughts of the creator', i.e. they were not created by any of the intermediaries created to create, but instead were thought of directly by the creator itself. For this reason, African people all over the continent value and respect plants in the deepest way, and this is especially seen in traditional societies where plants are valued as the most spiritual and mysterious of all life forms. I remember one occasion when an old Diola man and I were sitting beside a fire in the forest at dawn. The air was filled with the heavy scent of Parkia flowers and we were both immersed in our own thoughts, when suddenly the old man looked at me and remarked that with my interest in plants and creation, did I know that 'in plants we see the colours of creation and the creator and smell its beauty'.

TREE SPIRITS

Plants are the essence of life. They sustain us all, but their significance to Africans is far deeper. Their importance lies in their closeness to creation and hence their purity. They exist in their own sphere of time and are mysterious and dignified, possessing secrets that only a lucky few can understand. 'In the divine leaves we are able to find understanding of ourselves and our dreams,' an ancient woman plant diviner and healer from the Bassari ethnic group once said. To the Bassari, Malinke and Ibibio people, it is the wise who understand the rustle of leaves and the intimate connection between the wind and the trees. These communities often have sacred sites which include several old trees (usually Kapok) surrounding a freshwater pool, and it is believed that here the tree spirits can be 'met' by those who have the ability to communicate with them, and profound questions of life and death can be answered since trees retain the wisdom of eternal knowledge.

To traditional Africans, trees have souls, and these closely resemble those of other living creatures. In addition, trees can become the home of various ancestor spirits as well as the Foiro spirits. All plants with the exception of the wild tomato (*mentengo*), have a single, removable soul. Humans have two, the *Niyo* and *Kijo*, which can both emerge independently of the body at times. Plants have a *Niyo* which can emerge at certain times, such as in the middle of the day or during the night when it is said that 'plants move around'. However, the Kijo of plants is fixed within their structure and is represented by their shadow which can only move if the air spirits cause winds to rustle through the leaves. It is these rustlings that can be understood by plant diviners all over Africa, but especially in the west. The wild tomato is a special exception and according to the Bambara people of Mali, Senegal and Guinea, its *Kijo* or *Dya* is lodged with *Faro*, the god of water and one of the principal creators of the universe, where it is safe.

My first experience of tree spirits occurred when I was very small, when I made the journey into the forest on Aliou Diatta's back. I have since been back to the same spot and have had similar experiences. On the most recent occasion I returned with Aliou to consult the tree spirits before a long and potentially dangerous journey we were planning to make. As we rounded the last bend in the path we were faced by the clear forest pool that has been there as long as anyone can remember. Aliou pointed at some large fish as they swam away and noted how one of these rolled over in the water, exposing its left side. This he took as a sign that we should proceed towards the tree which was a few hundred metres away in the forest. Red Colobus monkeys crashed away overhead as we left the path and forged a way along a barely visible track. The tree was an awesome sight. It was immense; physically and spiritually a giant. It had a presence and seemed to hum as we approached.

We stopped on the edge of a cleared circle around the

tree. Aliou threw a red cola nut gently into the circle, and I followed with a white one. The atmosphere was electric. Something rustled in the undergrowth behind the tree, then bounded away. Suddenly and inexplicably there came a loud hollow-sounding 'Bam bam bam bam bam' from the tree. The sound grew in speed and intensity until we stepped back from the circle. The sound stopped immediately. When we approached it began again, and with each successive approach it increased. Aliou could not enter until the banging stopped. It was awesome and easily the most spectacular manifestation of nature that I have ever heard. We approached the tree seven times before Aliou was allowed to enter the circle and pour our offering of milk and wine on the stones and among the roots. Even during this the sound continued as a low rumble. We then each addressed the tree in turn, in Mandinka, asking it for advice. The forest around us was eerily silent. I became aware of every inch of my skin as it tingled in the strange electrical fashion that only a spirit presence can create. Sweat was rolling off Aliou's face in beads.

By now I could see clearly that this immense tree was solid and very healthy. It was not hollow. Its tall, straight trunk went up for forty or fifty metres, where its crown mingled with the others in the canopy. Aliou instructed me to stay in the circle while he returned to the pool to collect water. Being alone in the circle was strange. The tree buzzed while all the forest seemed quiet. Suddenly I felt quite overcome, as though I would faint. A pale greenish light seemed to descend from the canopy and enveloped the base of the tree, then swirled around the circle of stones and disappeared within the tree.

Suddenly Aliou was tugging at my arm and pointing at a scorpion which had appeared from nowhere. In my dizzy state I remember him reading its tracks as an answer to our questions. The scorpion was followed by a centipede which, by its sinuous movements, Aliou decided was in agreement with the scorpion. Our journey should be delayed by two days.

I remember thanking the tree through the haze and the light and wondering if they were one and the same. My body was tingling uncontrollably as I took some water and poured it around the circle of stones. We placed some palm nuts in the circle and stepped out backwards, being careful not to touch the stones. Suddenly the tree began to drum again, louder and louder, faster and faster. I remember stumbling away, following Aliou in an undignified retreat while the tree continued to drum. We stopped near the pool and listened to it for several more minutes before it ceased. The whole experience was inexplicable and powerful.

Aliou told me afterwards that he too had seen the greenish moving light and that it had actually circled me twice when I had entered into a daze. It had not wished to harm me Aliou told me, otherwise it would have killed me. We did delay our journey and the next day, the day on which we should have travelled, a rebel ambush killed many people at 7.00pm, the time we would have arrived in the town of Jarume. Jarume was to have been the stopping place on our journey and had we not been delayed we would almost certainly have been killed.

I have been to both this and other sacred sites since but have never been afforded as powerful a glimpse into the supernatural that we had that day. It was an amazing and unearthly experience and my respect for trees grew from that moment.

Leaf Masters

When plant spirits do emerge, they may make themselves known to humans through vivid dreams. In these encounters, the plant will demand that certain ceremonies are carried out in exchange for knowledge and the answers to specific questions. To the specialist plant diviner, the voice of a plant is as easily understood as that of a human. These so-called 'leaf masters' of Africa have been given the ability and wisdom to 'know' plants; these people are chosen by the plant itself. They will often belong to a family of leaf diviners in which at least one person from each generation has been chosen by the ancestral tree, in many cases a baobab, to carry on the tradition.

Of all Africa's diviners these leaf masters, *Jamba Tiyo* to the Pakao, are perhaps the most amazing. They become proficient in their art over many years and are normally taught much of what they know by their ancestral plant spirit. It all begins with a dream appearance by the tree spirit. In the dream the ancestral spirit indicates to the diviner-to-be that he or she has been chosen as the next person in the family to carry on the tradition of healing and learning. The apprentice will be told to go and pick a handful of leaves from another tree in the dream at a certain time and place the following day. Having done this and returned home with the bundle of leaves securely tied, they are placed in a special clay container and immediately a terrible illness strikes down the apprentice. For several days they will hover between life and death, oblivious to all around them. However, in this state their *Kijo* is taken into the forest by the ancestral spirit where it roams and is taught everything about the plant whose leaves were chosen. The period of learning may last only a day, or even a week or two, during which time the watching relatives will have to prepare certain foods to take to the ancestral tree, usually located in or near the village, where they will ask for the protection and safe return of the apprentice. Eventually, the *Jamba Tiyo* returns to this world and quickly recovers.

The knowledge they have gained so far becomes sacred and the next visitation is expected. When it comes, it may involve the picking of several types of leaf, followed by illness and another period of learning. It is said that the

Kijo of the *Jamba Tiyo* becomes progressively stronger and adapts to the spirit world and the world of plants. The first visit into this world can result in death since the human *Kijo* finds that world dangerous and it can be hard to breathe at first. Eventually though it becomes second nature and after several years of these journeys the experienced *Jamba Tiyo* can enter the world of plant spirits at will, and may even meet other leaf masters there.

An experienced leaf master usually resides in a small hut near or under their ancestral tree, from which they dispense advice and medicines to all who need them. They have a remarkable knowledge and appear to know why some people have come even before their symptoms have been explained. It must be remembered that in Africa, illnesses have both physical and spiritual causes and these must be treated accordingly. The leaf master can 'see' a person's ailment and through communication with the ancestral spirit will know what cures should be given. Plant parts used are chosen according to their spiritual properties, and a complex mixture of roots and leaves may be necessary to achieve the right cure. The plants must also grant permission for their use and can cause problems if this is not sought.

The actual procedure for the harvesting of plant parts is important and must be followed carefully. Plants must be picked from the west, then east, north then south. The digging and peeling of roots should also follow this procedure with each side attended to in order. During each stage the leaf master asks for the help of the universe (the space between the four cardinal points) in curing the sick person, while at times they will burn roots and leaves together 'in order to employ the spirit of fire' in the preparation.

Whenever I see a leaf master at work I am reminded that in Africa nothing is as it seems. A plant is never just a plant, or an animal just an animal. The world is full of transient spirits that, with the correct knowledge, can be harnessed to help humanity. We exist in a metaphysical world where a deeper knowledge waits to be discovered. Journeys into this world are not without danger but the rewards for those that survive and succeed are immense.

The Original Perfection of Creation

The importance of plants for humanity began when *Fonio*, the smallest seed, fell to the earth and spread the consciousness of the creator to all. To the Bambara and Dogon peoples of Mali the value of *Fonio* is immense. It is at once both the smallest and the greatest. In *Fonio* we hear the echoes of the past, and sitting in a field of these fragile plants listening to the wind it is truly possible to understand the spirituality of plants. *Fonio* 'is all the wisdoms' for the Balanta Kanja people. It is the embodiment of the creative spirit, the giver of life, the gentleness of being, the entwined fragility of life and death, for it is a weak, easily broken plant, yet strong enough to bend in the wind without breaking.

One reason why plants are believed to still be close to the original perfection of creation is due to *Faro* choosing a plant, rather than another life form, to protect the first earthly primordial twins. The most beautiful plant was chosen for both its wisdom and colour. It is a silvery colour in stem and leaf and is called *'Bama kung koyo'*, literally meaning 'the white-headed mother'. It was the 'mother' of the first twins of *Faro* and protected them when the flood waters rose at the beginning of the earth. *Bama kung koyo* is the first and the last, present throughout life, and used ceremonially at the time of death when its leaves are placed in the grave of the deceased. It is said that the colour of the leaves and their fragrant smell encourage the Aboule spirits to take the soul of the deceased into the 'forest of happiness'. The rustling of the leaves at the graveside is believed to call the spirits. In death we are therefore reunited with the perfection of the original creation through the intercession of one of the first plants.

The Wisdom of Plants

The wisdom of plants is everywhere. We exist in their shade and are lucky if we can learn something from them. To the Mankanye people of Guinea Bissau, the tree is life. Every village has its sacred tree where it is said the ancestors gather to talk. This tree is usually an old mahogany and is often gnarled with buttress roots. A space is cleared around the tree and a row of low stakes is placed in a circle (around the tree). There are usually twenty-two stakes (sometimes stones), representing the spirals of thought used during the creation. At a point in front of the tree is placed a new clay pot, bottom end up. This is the 'table of the spirits' on which food is placed before requests are made of them. To the initiated, the tree oracle is the greatest, and the most powerful leaf masters are able to hear the voice of the tree. It is a representation of the creator, encircled by the points of creation and humanity, in the form of those that have come for advice.

Every country has its magic plants and trees, and it is also said that every person has their own special tree. You may often have seen a particular tree in dreams or felt a liking for one while out walking. In Africa, my tree is the wonderful Koutouboolo, with its dark fruits that may be used to make an indigo dye.

EXERCISE

Iri Boro Deda (Creating a Tree Medicine)

◆ Take some twigs from your favourite tree, a hazel for example. Pick them in the spring when they are full of energy. An equivalent period in Africa is the onset of the rains.

◆ Bind the twigs together with a strand of wild mallow bark. In Africa it would be the bark of the 'Dajilo', a common rainy season plant.

◆ Take your bundle of twigs to a quiet spot. Anoint them with a little water, then alcohol and milk, and with each libation direct your thoughts towards the spirit of the tree from which you took the twigs. Ask for advice or help.

◆ Close your eyes and concentrate totally on the leaves of the plant, then its trunk. Try and become the whorls on the trunk; imagine you are blowing in the breeze, absorbing the energy of the wind. Enter as much as you can into feeling what it is like to be that tree. Ask its help through the bundle of twigs. Be sincere and honour it, and it will do the same for you.

◆ When you have finished, anoint the twigs again, with milk only this time. Take them home and put them in a place where they can dry.

- On the third day if you are a man, the fourth if you are a woman, take the bundle of twigs out. It should be dry by now. Add a little of your favourite scented oil. Then burn the twigs while placing your wishes into the smoke.

- At the end, carefully collect the ashes and take them back to the original tree where you got the twigs. Approach the tree slowly and thank it for allowing its twigs to be used. Then rub the ashes into the trunk while asking for the continued help of the tree in the future.

- Whenever you pass the tree always acknowledge it and remember to touch it sometimes, especially when making requests. Take note of any thoughts or dreams you may have in which the tree of your choice appears. Also note other dreams you may have which include a greenish light that moves in the breeze.

- Treat the tree you have chosen with reverence and it will help you to grow spiritually.

Once you know the individual properties of trees it is possible to blend them and burn twigs of different types. The various spiritual properties of leaves, bark and twigs can then be harnessed. The whole learning process is a long one and requires perseverance, but once the knowledge of plants is achieved it is immensely valuable. The spiritual powers of plants are never ending, and this is their greatest wisdom.

4

THE WISDOM OF LIFE
AND DEATH

For African people, life is a never-ending cycle; it may
be thought of as an oval bounded on all sides by time
and space. Our lives and deaths are ultimately linked with
the original oval, or 'egg of the world', which bounds our
universe and is the limit of perfection. Our short and
fragile lives are merely one part of the cycle which links
us ultimately to the primordial notion of twins, in this
case life and death, who belong together, or are at least
inextricably linked.

DEATH AND REBIRTH

African peoples have an unrivalled acceptance of death,
though it is viewed with deep suspicion since it will
always be wholly unnatural in the created order of things.
This suspicion stems from the time during the creation

when the nefarious activities of flawed spiritual beings led to the downfall of humanity from its position of eminence close to the creator. This downgrading of humanity was usually the result of trickery of one sort or another and humans remain bitter and opposed to death even today.

From death there has emerged a strong pragmatism, however, and each African society has developed beliefs which can be beneficial to people everywhere in understanding the roles of life and death, especially since death (in many societies) is often viewed as a tragedy or an end. To traditional Africans death is a beginning. As certainly as one body dies, so another is reborn. The means by which this happens may seem difficult to understand, though in reality it is simple. To grasp this knowledge what is first required is an understanding of the spiritual nature of a human body. The Mandinka tradition is perhaps the easiest to explain.

The Spiritual Nature of the Human Body

At birth we are without a soul. However, an ancestor soul has been allocated to each new-born and this, the *Kijo* or *Dya*, enters the child almost as soon as it is born into the world. This soul aspect is always from an ancestor of the opposite sex. *Faro*, the god of water, keeps these soul aspects safe in the water while they await rebirth. The *Kijo* is the aspect of the soul that acts almost as a double. It wanders while we sleep, for example, and our dreams are the result of its adventures and the dangers it may have faced. As in our world, there are wild animals and people of dubious character that can attempt to capture the *Kijo* for their own purposes.

A second soul aspect is called the *Niyo*. Again, a new-born lacks this part and a beautiful ceremony is carried out to ensure that a *Niyo* enters the child, as it contains an important aspect which will determine the character of the baby. This character is known as the *Tere* and it comes with the *Niyo*.

The Naming Ceremony

A few days after a baby is born (three days for a boy and four for a girl), the special soul naming ceremony is held, often under the village sacred tree. Traditionally, this ceremony is carried out by the most respected people in the village, an old man and an old woman. The ceremony usually takes place at night, by star and fire light, those two great symbols of the perfection that was the beginning of time. The child is held up to each of the cardinal points of the universe, which is asked to bless the life of the child and its name. The baby is then named, usually after one of its ancestors whose *Tere* it is believed to have inherited. At this point the *Niyo* of an ancestor is believed to enter the baby and will remain with it through life. The baby's head is then shaved, half of the hair being placed in a new clay pot which is sealed and kept in the house. The other half is then taken to the river and thrown into the water 'since *Faro* still controls the *Kijo* of the child, some of which symbolically resides in the hair'.

The old woman then washes the baby in milk, millet beer and water, anointing it in the purity of these liquids which will surround it in life. The *Kijo*, which has been dormant since entering the baby at birth, is now activated by the *Niyo* and it is believed that the baby is free to dream and develop. Together, these two spiritual parts of the child will control its life and try to ensure its well being in all things. The *Tere* interacts with the other two soul aspects and can in time influence them for good or bad. After a person dies it is believed that their *Tere* can become vengeful if their character was not good in life, and such a vengeful spirit can inflict harm on living relatives.

This beautiful naming ceremony aptly illustrates the role of the ancestors in everyday life. It is a moment in a baby's life when it is in touch with the perfection of the universe, its community, which is united in wishing it well, and above all the ancestors, which are believed to be gathered all around during the naming ceremony. It is a supreme moment when the baby is surrounded only by goodness, purity and love.

The Approach of Death

Death, however, is just as important as birth, but far more traumatic for the relatives as well as for the *Niyo* and *Kijo* of the deceased. As a person approaches death, through illness for example, their *Kijo* begins to wander, often far away. It hovers near the dying body, and intermittently returns to it to associate with the *Niyo* which remains inside until the actual moment of physical death. The period during which the *Kijo* hovers near the body can be several days, during which time it makes progressively longer journeys away from the body. When it returns to the body it reports back and helps calm the *Niyo* to prevent the dying person feeling afraid. Often at this stage, the dying person may be aware of other people in the room, since the *Kijo* is taking over the emotions of the dying person and preparing them. The *Kijo* may call ancestor spirits to the bedside of the dying person, both to comfort and encourage them.

There may also be appearances by the magical lights known to the Balanta people as Aboule (good spirits). At this time they become visible to the dying person as a transition is being made between this life and the next. As death approaches, the Aboule and prominent ancestors gather around since this is a vulnerable moment for the *Niyo* which must emerge intact from the body. It may be thought of as a second birth, spiritual in every sense. Just as there are dangers in physical birth, so there are in spiritual birth. For the dying person, the last memory is of a bright light, often yellow, blue or even pale green. This is the moment when the *Kijo* and *Niyo* 'see together' for an instant, then the *Niyo* is in the arms of Aboule who will help it. Both the *Niyo* and the *Kijo* feel the suffering of the living relatives, and the *Niyo* especially will feel a lot of pain and loneliness for a time. Once the Aboule are sure that the *Niyo* is safe they leave it hovering near the body where it will remain until burial.

Shortly before death it is regarded as natural for the *Kijo* to appear to certain living relatives or friends. It may announce itself to a friend of the deceased who had no idea that their friend was dying. The *Kijo* is also able to make itself visible for a very short time *after* death, though the actual length of time of any appearance may be brief. This is believed to be dependent on the strength of character (*Tere*) that the deceased had in life. A person with a strong character may appear several times to different people, even over a period of a few days, but a person of normal character appears only to one or two very close friends or relatives. It does this to warn them of what has happened and to comfort them. The *Kijo* can reveal itself as it was in life or it may appear with the light of the Aboule spirits who transform it soon after death and take it to the water or forest where it will be safe and await rebirth.

The *Niyo*

The presence of the *Niyo* around the dead body ensures that grief does not prevent the mourners and relatives carrying out the correct burial procedures. These are very important if the *Niyo* is to feel reassured that it is not forgotten. The *Niyo* follows the procession to the grave and before that to any ceremonies at which the corpse may be questioned. In such a case, the *Niyo* directs the body in answer to questions concerning its death, especially if murder may have been carried out. The *Niyo* 'sees all' once it has left the body, and if there was any foul play it will know the culprit. If there was foul play and the *Niyo* is *not* given the opportunity to declare its views then it may become angry, and in this state it cannot prepare itself for eventual rebirth at some time in the future. Such spirits are known as *N'foura* and are extremely dangerous to living relatives.

However, if all has gone well, the *Niyo* begins to associate with other ancestral spirits. They have their own hierarchy in which they reside until such time as they may be reborn. They rest a lot of the time, following a long, hard life, but their principal role is in protecting living relatives by advising them in times of crisis. Rarely do they appear in a person's waking state as this would probably frighten a person too much and could even precipitate their early demise; more often they appear in dreams either in their human form or in the form of the totem animal of the family. They will advise of any present crises and can foretell the future. Following a visitation, it is important to play the favourite music of the ancestor (*see* Chapter 5) and to provide its favourite food. Any instructions it has made should also be carried out. Food and wine are left in special sacred places which are maintained regularly.

Sacred Sites or Shrines

In Senegal, the Balanta, Manjack, Papel, and Mankanye peoples have similar ceremonies and sacred sites for the ancestors. A site is chosen, in the forest or in a garden, where three or four stones are laid out, depending on the gender of the ancestor. At other times seven stones may be laid out representing the perfection of the male and female twins of the primordial creation; they may also symbolise the sexual neutrality of the ancestors after death. The stones are laid in a circle in the middle of which is a small gourd or calabash, buried so that only its open end is visible. In this, water and wine are placed for the ancestor to imbibe symbolically. Inside the circle and next to the gourd is placed a small flat stone, the table of the ancestors, on which food is placed for the spirit. Some shrines have a small roof erected over them to protect them from the elements. It is important to always maintain a shrine that has been set up. It is a site of enormous importance and if neglected will cause great distress to the ancestor it represents.

It is also possible to set up a larger shrine which will

represent several ancestors. Fourteen, or even twenty-two stones, may be placed in the circle since there were twenty-two spirals of thought in the first creation. The essential aspect of the shrine is that it contains the food and liquid necessary for the survival of the ancestral spirit(s). In consulting such a shrine, talk to it as if it is a person you can see. This gradually becomes easier, especially when advice is given in dreams and a familiarity is built up with the shrine and its spirits. To those who are experienced, the ancestors may occasionally appear during the day, at the time of consultation or at home.

On a cautionary note it is extremely important not to blunder into a ghost, catching it unawares. Since they live near shrines, always announce your presence. In a startled state, a ghost can momentarily envelop a person in its mist, reducing them instantly to madness. This is common in Africa and is sometimes termed 'bush spirit madness'. Ghosts do not want to harm humans and choose times of day to move around when there are few people about. In the hottest part of the day, when most people are resting, a ghost can turn up almost anywhere. These African ghosts are 'like a rapidly moving mist that glides over the ground in an upright form'. They can move at a surprisingly fast speed and seem to appear from nowhere. They often retreat into the holes in giant trees or between buttress roots. If the face of the ghost can be seen it can be identified, but since they are so dangerous to humans they avoid contact wherever possible.

Eventually, the ghost fades and can no longer be seen

by ordinary people, though they can still appear in dreams or be contacted by a *kunfun* (spirit musician). The spirit remains in contact and near its living relatives, however.

The Death of a Baby

There is another category of life and death. This is the situation in which a woman has a number of miscarriages, still births or babies who die soon after birth. In these cases it is said that 'the *Kijo* does not want to be born'; in effect, it has refused to come back. It is an unhappy situation for the parents, who must contact their ancestors to ascertain the cause of the problem. A short ceremony is carried out at the village sacred tree, usually in conjunction with a leaf master or other spiritual leader, at which millet, couscous and beer are presented to the ancestors. Once the problem has been identified the correct action can then be taken to ensure that the *Kijo* of the next child conceived will not be allowed to depart without good reason.

Mementoes of the Deceased

Death and dying are never easy for humans to understand. We feel the pain of the dying and the departed feel our pain. It is important for both parties to move on, though this can seem incredibly hard. In Africa it is common for relatives to carry a memento of the person who has died and it is believed that this allows an essence of the person to remain with you at all times. Since hair contains important soul elements and does not disintegrate easily it is often incorporated into charms and necklaces, and this is one of the most effective ways of staying in touch and deriving the protection that a deceased person can give.

After the formalities, take the hair and place it with a small piece of wood and a fresh shoot from your favourite tree. Wrap these together in leaves, again preferably from your chosen tree, and tie them together with spiders' webs. Take a small pebble (choose the colour and size by intuition). Touch this briefly against the leaves and make a spiritual connection. Then take the bundle of leaves and bury them somewhere significant where you will pass often and always remember; in front of the door is often a good place. As you bury the bundle of leaves you can pour a little water on it and add a blessing and a wish, since water is for journeys, purity and the protection of God. Then bury the bundle but always carry the stone. Never lose it; it is part of an eternal memory. Each time you pass the place where the bundle is buried acknowledge it in thought.

In the Balanta religion there is no heaven. The spirits remain near us and if we acknowledge them they act as guardians and advisers. The pebble represents the circle of life and is a repository of dreams and memories. Sleep with it under your pillow sometimes and you may dream the beautiful dreams of the dead, when the past, present and future are one and from which you can wake reassured that everything is well for both yourself and the deceased. Be free, do not be afraid. Just remember there is life we can see and life which is less visible, but it is all life, all part of the energy of the creator.

Traditional Africans make offerings to a whole host of spirits and ancestors. Sacred places where offerings are made include forest pools, caves, strange rock formations, large bodies of water, crossroads, the earth, and the universe. If we respect the sacred spaces of the earth we will always be able to hear the wisdom of the past, and understand the eternal cycle and our place within it. With this understanding comes a courage that enables us to live our lives and to understand death in a way that makes it less traumatic.

In the reflection of still waters we can see the continuity of life and in rings of stones we can understand the permanence of being, in one form or another. African wisdom is the wisdom of knowing how we can use colour, stones and music in the most profound ceremonies that echo across time, carrying the message of truth, rebirth and renewal. Add to these a respect for the soul and an understanding of the endless cycles linked to the 'egg of the world', and there is a wisdom that is ancient and still alive. This is the true value and wisdom of life and death in Africa.

5

THE WISDOM OF
MUSIC

In many ways, music may be seen as the 'soul' of Africa.
It is everywhere, both formally at social occasions, and
informally with children making and playing their own
instruments in small groups for the sheer love of it. Music
is the magical essence of every African society and is at
the heart of all truth and knowledge. Music is the oldest
created thing, emerging at the beginning of time in the
first vibrations that emanated from the emptiness. Music
is part of the *mana*, or life force, that permeates all things,
and it possesses its own essence of the creator in a way
that nothing else does. In Africa music is an integral part
of most spiritual ceremonies and rituals and its resonance
pulsates in the hearts of people in every part of the continent. From the driest deserts to the deepest forests, music
is adored and played with passion and energy.

The variety of musical instruments in Africa is extraordinary. Some of the most amazing are the most simple;

the most stirring music I ever heard was a duet between two Balanta friends, one playing the three-holed bamboo flute, the other playing the one-stringed *kambalaon*, a strange instrument that is played with both fingers and mouth at once. The gentle tones of the flute and the strange buzzing of the *kambalaon* seemed to blend with the falling of the sun and the approaching dusk. Listening to these two musicians I truly felt that these instruments were as much a part of Africa as the crickets, cicadas and other musical insects that fill the air with sound, day and night.

THE SPIRITUAL ESSENCE OF MUSIC

However, music in Africa is more than just an aggregation of sounds played for fun. It is a spiritual essence that permeates every gathering. It is even said that 'every spirit and ancestor has its favourite music'.

The Naming Ceremony

Music is said to 'help the first aspects of the human character to develop', and for this reason music and dance are an important part of a baby's naming ceremony. To the sound of drums, tambourines and rattles, the village elder approaches the new-born baby and lifts it up. The instruments fall silent, though the *kambalaon* continues its mysterious buzz. The elder looks intently into the eyes of the baby, then notes it hair, facial features and wrinkles before holding it up to the sky with its myriad stars. As the baby is held to each cardinal point it is asked for the blessing of the universe throughout its life. The baby is given its name and the *balafone* (an African xylophone) and *kambalaon* join each other in a haunting tune that seems as old as time itself. The notes are said to 'rise and fall as gently as a baby's breath' and they welcome both the child's character (*Tere*) and its soul (*Niyo*).

In celebration, women begin to dance; a circle forms around the elder and baby, and drums begin to roll into the African night in the ancient rhythm of the 'soul calling' tune. An old woman shaves the child's head as a musician strikes up with the three-holed bamboo flute. This ceremony signifies that the naming is complete and the festivities can begin in earnest. Musical instruments of all varieties are brought out in celebration of the completion of this most sacred and important act. I believe it is immensely significant that music plays such an important part in this ceremony, as it instils in the baby the spirituality that it will have throughout its life. The music played mingles with the soul *and* character aspects that have been called and begins the development process in a profound and beautiful way.

Contacting Spirits through Music

At such social gatherings many musical instruments may be used, and one of the most interesting is the mysterious 'earth bow', which booms from the earth and is said to call the souls of the ancestors and other earth spirits to the aid of humanity. I have seen the musicians actually use music to contact the ancestral and other spirits which are then consulted for advice which the living need to hear. It has been said to me many times that all spiritual beings adore music. It is part of the creative make-up of all living beings and all things are said to possess their own music and vibration that began during the creation and is the foundation of life itself. There is the music of plants, rocks, streams, rivers, even the stars and universe, and there is the music of the earth and all the spirits.

It is also said that 'there is music that all can hear and music that is only audible to the *kunfun* who has the duty of listening and translating'. In one of the most mysterious interactions, a *kunfun* may be woken in the night by his or her ancestral spirit playing a tune in a dream. This tune is special to the musician and he or she will understand the signal and wake up. For the Balanta people, the music in the dream is always played on the *balafone*. The *kunfun* gets up, and without saying anything to anyone gently begins to play the tune he or she has just heard being played. At this moment, the ancestral spirit glides into the room 'like smoke'. Gradually, though, a human form is assumed and a conversation will take place in which the ancestor may warn of things that may bring danger to the village and will advise on issues that may be troubling family members. Messages will be given which the *kunfun* will later pass on. In some cases, the ancestor will announce that a village elder will soon die. Although the elder in question is not told, this news is helpful since it gives time for the family to prepare.

Problem-solving and the *kunfun*

Ancestral spirits are able to communicate with the *kunfun* in much the same way that plant spirits communicate with the leaf masters. The *kunfun* will have learned the music of each ancestor and each relevant plant or animal spirit over many years. These can be employed to help people who come with problems and illnesses of many kinds. The *kunfun* will also work closely with leaf masters and other African spiritualists and may refer patients to these if the spirits contacted by music suggest this course of action.

When a person comes to the musician for help they enter a special room in which the *balafone* is kept and where the sacred tunes are played. The musician plays the music of his closest ancestral guide and it is not long before the spirit makes its appearance and will begin to communicate with the musician. It is a mysterious situation to watch, with the musician in deep conversation with a being that is usually unseen by everyone else, though in some cases it may be heard. I should mention as well that the musician does not go into a trance or dance frantically to induce a meeting with the ancestor. It is simply a polite conversation between two friends who have things to ask each other. The ancestral spirit may at this stage advise that the musician contact another spirit for help, and he or she will be given the relevant tune to play to call this entity.

When I have attended these meetings I have always been profoundly moved by the encounter. They are simplistic and beautiful, and the meeting may last for up to half an hour, during which time the musician occasionally stops to play the *balafone* or the three-holed flute as this is said to 'make the spirit happy'. The tiny spirit flute is made of thin bamboo with the ends blocked and three holes bored into the top.

If the musician plays to call another, non-ancestral spirit, he or she closes their eyes and sways gently. The firelight flickers as the notes appear to hang in the air with a resonant quality that is purely spiritual and hard to describe. When the musician has finished he or she puts down the flute and stares intently into the darkness, face beaded in sweat and eyes focused in concentration. Remember that this is not an ancestral spirit appearing and it may take a horrible form. Despite this, the musician begins to talk in a soft voice that blends with the semi-darkness and the smell of smoke from the wood fire. The spirit that is present will advise on the problem in question and may offer help itself, or may refer the person onto a *Dano* who understands animal spirits, or a *Jamba Tiyo* who understands the spirit of plants.

In other cases, the spirit may advise the playing of music to appease the entities causing the problems and so solve them. These very African musicians are extremely useful in determining the cause of illnesses and they play a profound 'music of the soul' that reaches far beyond the realms of our world into the spirit world that only a privileged few can truly understand. It is impossible to watch these gentle interactions with the spirit world without being intensely moved by the simplicity and purity as well as the honesty of it all.

Music and Mediums

Music and mediums of all kinds are intricately linked to each other. They exist in parallel, almost symbiotic worlds, where one person plays the magical instrument while another is led by it into other dimensions of time and space. There are musicians for every occasion. Some of the greatest are the travelling *Griots* of West Africa, who sing profound songs and 'know all things'. They wander, singing of past heroes, kings, storytellers, or of those great oracles who could divine better than anyone else. These amazing musicians appear to 'talk' to their instruments and the replies correspond in every way (in intonation) to the musicians' voices. Together they 'speak' and large crowds gather to hear them. The startling tonal qualities of simple instruments such as the one-stringed violin of West Africa are amazing, and in the hands of a master musician they appear to have a life of their own.

The Funeral Ceremony

Music is also played at funerals and before and after death. The Balanta people play a *balafone* using two players, usually younger members of the deceased person's family. They play special pieces of music for the deceased so that it will know that it is not forgotten. At the graveside, the music of the *balafone* mingles with the cries of birds and monkeys in the forest and joins the hum of the cicadas in the heat. In these circumstances the true spiritual essence of African music can best be appreciated. Its wisdom is in linking all facets of this life, and to this life is linked the universe, profound and deep with its own gentle hum 'like the murmur of faraway voices mingled with running water'.

EXERCISE

Fenba Dari (A Universal Request)

Music can put us in touch with ourselves in any country or situation; I only have to hear the buzzing of the *kambalaon* to be carried away. It is easy to meditate if you find the right music.

♦ Choose the music for the situation. For me the African zithers or kora harp are full of magic.

♦ Go to a place that is special to you, for example a tree shrine if you have set one up.

♦ Take a small sample of earth from each of the four cardinal points. As you do so ask for the help of the universal creator, the beings who inhabit the worlds attached to each cardinal point and the spiritual world that is close to us. Remember there is a world of energy around us.

♦ Take a small piece of bark from each side of the special tree you have chosen. It is important that bark or leaves are harvested from west to east then north to south. Again repeat your requests as you do this.

- Take some coal or charcoal and make a small fire until you have some glowing coals.

- Take a coloured cloth, again use your intuition at the time and allow for the fact that the colour can vary on different occasions when you participate in this ceremony.

- Place the four pieces of bark on the cloth in east, west, south and north positions. On each piece of bark place a small amount of the soil until it is divided equally between the four.

- Play the music you have previously chosen, close your eyes and imagine you are travelling between the four cardinal points against the background of blue, red, green or yellow. Let the music take you into other planes of thought, and ask the universe, the ancestors, and the spirits of nature for help and blessings in this life. Ask that they will open your mind fully to greater understanding and especially that they will help you to dream and through dreaming acquire greater knowledge.

- If you play a musical instrument yourself you can use this to create the atmosphere of thought. By intuition you will know what to play and how to play it and you may find yourself carried into the inner beauty of the mind and soul. You will know when to stop.

- Pour a little water on each piece of bark and soil. Carefully gather these in the order in which you placed them on the table. One by one, throw each sample of soil towards its cardinal point.

- Dig a small hole and in this place the pieces of bark one on top of the other. Add the glowing coals, then take some water and pour it onto the coals. As the steam rises, blow it towards the four cardinal points, but while some remains quickly put soil onto the coals so that some steam is trapped in the earth. This symbolically unites you with the earth. Its energies will always be with you, guiding and advising. Your thoughts have entered the sky through the steam and the soil thrown to the four cardinal points.

This exercise will open your mind to dreams and to the fantastic blue, white, red and gold 'thoughts' that are all around, waiting to help us when we are completely ready in thought and deed. Believe in what you are doing and it will be your companion and guide.

The Music of Creation

Music has been with me since I was small. The pounding of drums and the strumming of harps and zithers has always freed my mind, yet there is also a beautiful music in the forest. It is the eternal, pure music of spiritual perfection, understood by crickets and cicadas as well as certain people. I was once taken on a journey into the forest at dusk. The noisy clamour of the day had given way to the owls, frogs, bats and hyenas which called in the distance. Not too far away a lion gave its 'oooooohhhh' call. The old woman guiding me led me to a place in the forest where a tree had fallen, leaving a gap in the canopy. Here we waited in the silence for a time, absorbing all the sounds around us. The old woman explained how we dream and where dreams come from. She told me of her dreams of stars and the moon and pointed up towards the sky. 'Each star is a life,' she said, 'and there, look at that star falling.' She pointed excitedly at a streak across the sky. 'That is the expiry of a bad person, they have lost their glittering star.'

The old woman took some bark and leaves and made a small fire which smelt sweet and aromatic. When this had gone out completely she took the ashes, mixed them with water and began to paint my face with the lines and marks of creation, the stars and planets. When she had finished she spoke again. 'Now listen to the music of the forest, and listen to the music of the sky.' We sat in silence in the stillness. At first all I could hear were crickets and bats and the occasional nocturnal primate clicking. Then there it was, a faint distant hum, a buzzing that was so gentle it made me want to float on it, to drift away. The moon began to rise above the trees, bathing us in a silvery light. I took some water as instructed and poured it on the hands of the old woman, and she then held her hands to the moon and blessed it in a soft voice that blended with the other sounds all around.

My body buzzed with the atmosphere of it all. The clearing we were in seemed to come alive with magic and an ethereal beauty that made me stand up. I was suddenly surrounded by the most beautiful music, natural and pure. Even the moon seemed to give off its own sound, a gentle faraway buzzing and whispering. 'Listen,' the old woman instructed me, 'that is the music of creation, the whispers in time.' It could indeed be described as whispers, but these were whispers that passed over and through your mind and soul and echoed in your thoughts. The moon finally began to disappear over the clearing edge and we made our way back along the narrow path towards the village. The lion called again, closer this time, and was mocked in reply by the moan of a hyena. We stopped and I washed my face.

'Tonight I have shown you something utterly rare and precious' she said. 'You must never tell anyone of it until I have gone from this life, you must promise me that. Now go on in your life, remember what you have seen and especially what you have heard. Never doubt and if you do, remember this night when the sky played for you, the universe is with you. Learn to dream with it.' Then she was gone, shuffling away into the darkness. I stood for a few moments looking at the sky which was now silent again, then I too went into my room here I hoped I would dream of the lights of bright stars, but on that occasion at least, it was not to be.

I will be eternally grateful to that old woman for showing me something so sacred and profound. Sadly she died recently, and I am now able to share the deep spiritual experience of that night more widely. I have often stood and looked at the stars and moon but never again have I felt the magic and heard the gentle whispering. That old woman was magic herself; she had the ability to conjure profound dreams from the abstract and she was able to teach me to hear the stars and the universe.

Music itself can also take us into dimensions of thought where beautiful things can be learned and appreciated. The truly experienced spirit musicians have even learned the music of the stars. The gentle rhythms of this deep spirit music engender a peace and tranquillity that can hardly be described. It is more than just sound; it is within and all around, it is light and simplicity, purity and ancient love all rolled into one. That is the true wisdom of African music, now and always.

6

EARTH WISDOM

To the traditional African person, there are two great sources of life: the earth and its waters, which originally emanated from the universe during the creation. In fact, in many societies in Africa the earth is the closest thing that people have to a concept of 'God'. Things are changing, however, and outside influences have often introduced concepts of a universal God which did not exist before. To people who still adhere to the old ways, the earth is 'like a parent', the source of all life and substance, the perpetual creator of new life. It is filled with mystery and magic and contains worlds that we as humans can barely understand since they are so different from what we ourselves know.

'THE EGG OF THE WORLD'

The earth hangs in the original space before time. It is a part of the 'egg of the world', the giant sphere that encapsulates us and our universe. In the Balanta concept, we and our earth are one of the three layers that make up this giant egg. The earth and the universe are inextricably linked, bound together by the past. It is a spiritual as well as a physical union. This is why the traditional concept of the earth shows it as having seven layers (*see* page 77). These layers are linked forever to the four worlds that have existed since time and creation began, and there will, it is believed, be other worlds in the future. I must add that most people can only see the earth in its physical terms; however, there are people in Africa who are specialists in all things that concern the earth. They are masters at seeing and understanding, and form close links with the other 'spiritualists', such as those that understand plants and animals.

The Aboule

The earth was created long ago by the spirits. In the Balanta religion, the *Boisee*, the creative spirits are called Aboule. They may roughly be equated with the European concept of angels, though they do not normally appear in human form and are recognised by their translucent electric blue colour that is described by those who have seen them as 'unlike any colour on this earth'. The Aboule are believed to have been created at the beginning of time when the universal creative force, *Gla* to the Bambara people, needed help in creation. There was so much to be done that the Aboule were instructed to take part, spreading out far and wide, each with their own task, and they set the universe vibrating with life and sound. They helped carry the seed of consciousness which became humanity and carried out the difficult task of creating the earth itself with all its diverse intricate life forms. When worlds were created wrongly they were recreated again later (hence we are in the fourth world). The Aboule may therefore be regarded as the emissaries of the original creation and they have retained a special interest in the affairs of humanity to this day.

The Spiritual Earth

The earth is alive and is regarded as all sustaining, all seeing, the source of all life, dreams and spiritual beings. As my adviser Aliou Diatta once told me, 'there is no heaven, only earth'. Heaven is a vague concept to people such as Aliou. When we die we remain on the earth, though we are all represented by a star which shines brightly for the good and fades gradually into invisibility for those that are bad or who fail in this life. I believe this concept of the bright or pale star illustrates the link that the earth and its inhabitants retain with the universe and the 'egg'. In death we are allowed the vision that we lack in life; to see and understand the beauty of the 'spiritual earth'. In life we can at best accept that the earth is alive and give it the respect that it deserves. To followers of the traditional religions the earth is as alive as you or I, and it is alive with an intense power. In trying to describe this idea, Aliou compares the power of the earth in relation to humanity in terms of our power in relation to that of an ant.

Many traditional societies have viewed the earth as divine or sacrosanct, and belief in its being alive is perhaps not surprising in the African context. The earth *is* alive and is believed to possess ears, eyes and a mouth. The lungs of the earth enable it to breathe and its fertility derives straight from the creative elements given to it in the past. All life on earth exists at the mercy and whim of the spiritual forces in the soil and its underground tributaries and streams. Earth souls and spirits may be found in a number of different places, such as in caves, between crevices in rocks and under boulders.

Soba

In traditional African religions, the earth is ruled by its own God, *Soba* in the Bambara religion of *Mali*. *Soba* is in overall control and rules over a whole host of other entities which are living on or in the earth but are not directly part of it, i.e. they are not its souls. *Soba* is good, somewhat distant from humanity but able to feel compassion and mercy, especially if humans and animals are persecuted by unjust earth spirits. *Soba* requires offerings of food and wine as well as songs and dances, and in exchange will ensure that rains will fall and crops will flourish.

Earth Shrines

Earth shrines dedicated to this purpose are common in West Africa. Normally a small corner of a field will be set aside. There a post is planted into the ground, and this marks the point where offerings of food and wine are made before planting and the harvest. The owner of the field may also pray for protection from wild animals such as snakes and scorpions which may be sent by nefarious entities. A simple shrine like this is a poignant reminder of our fragility in the face of nature. It is also a reminder that we are surrounded by beings far greater than us, and it is only through alliances which we maintain that we can flourish and grow spiritually.

EXERCISE

Boisé n'din (The Small Sacred Space)

♦ To set up one of these shrines cut a sapling with a fork at one end. This should be your chosen tree. The piece should be about a metre long.

♦ Gently strip the bark off and allow the wood to dry.

♦ Take a piece of coloured cloth, again it should be of your own choice; your favourite colour will be fine.

♦ If you are a woman, find four medium-sized, round, flattish stones; if male then take three.

♦ Find a quiet place, such as in the corner of your garden, and put the wood in the ground. Tie the coloured cloth around the top of the stick, just below the fork, then take the stones and place them around the base of the stick so that they are touching. Pour water around the stones, and a little alcohol onto to them.

♦ Close you eyes and ask the spirits of the earth to centre on this place. Tell them that you will afford them honour and respect and ask them in return for their help, advice and knowledge.

♦ Place some food on one of the flat stones. Never eat in the presence of the stones without offering food to them. This may be a symbolic gesture but it is very important.

Once you have set up a shrine it must be maintained. Do not ignore it. Never contact the shrine in the middle of the day, however. At this time the spirits rest and must not be disturbed, the evening or early morning is best. Always bring milk and food when you come, and keep the area clean and sacred. Do not allow anyone but yourself to touch the stones or the stick.

This shrine symbolically links you to the earth and the spirits that live in it. Special care should be taken not to kill any living thing within sight of the shrine as this would be very bad luck. The forked stick represents the two souls of humanity rooted in the past and dependent on the earth then as now. We cannot escape this dependency at any stage. The colour of the cloth is significant since it represents the colour of the earth spirit. These simple shrines embody simplicity and purity and advise their owners through thought and by dreams. Do not be afraid to dream of them or to find yourself next to the shrine during your dream. If this happens then be aware and follow any instructions you are given.

I have been to these types of shrines many times. They are often consulted before planting and harvesting, and in these cases may be offered part of the harvest. They can be immensely atmospheric, especially when located in small clearings in the forest. It is here that yams are often grown and at times their tendrils may wrap themselves around the stick in a beautiful union between physical and spiritual dimensions. I have found incredible peace

when I have had the opportunity to sit on the bare earth in front of one of these shrines. With the gentle rustling of the trees overhead and the occasional call of birds and squirrels the shrine has a calming effect on the human spirit. At night these places are equally calm, and on starlit nights are immensely beautiful. I see such places as the true embodiment of nature, both spiritual and meta-physical. Here the two worlds blend into a green world of sound and sensation that is indescribable. It is a privilege to enter such a world and I hope that you will derive the same calmness and beauty from it as I have.

The Seven Layers of the Earth

The Balanta and Mandinka people believe the earth has seven layers, each inhabited by different beings. However, the beautiful seventh earth (layer) is the home of dead children. Here they are taught by special beings who prepare them for eventual rebirth when they are ready. These beings are the 'lights of the earth' and are believed to be adorned in the most beautiful colours. At times an earth being will appear in dreams to the parents of deceased children. They advise of the child's progress and happiness in the seventh earth. It is extremely comforting for distressed parents to have such a visitation, and it is even more beautiful when the 'child of light' accompanies the earth being to visit its parents.

Earth Spiritualists and Water Diviners

The earth is very beautiful, very mysterious and also dangerous. There are quiet waters where we cannot walk and deep forests where we cannot see. We exist bounded by our fragile emotions, seeing some things but missing so much. The earth spiritualists and water diviners 'see and understand' and exert a powerful charismatic magnetism toward anyone who has met them. In my own estimation the earth spiritualists are as incredible as the African water seekers (diviners), who use no sticks, only their bare feet.

It is said that when you call a well digger you must also call a water seeker, as one knows the spirits of the earth and the dangers he will face while digging, and the other understands the spirits of the underground water sources.

First of all, the well digger takes a back seat in the shade while the seeker gets to work. Shuffling along slowly the seeker 'looks into the soil'. (Remember that seekers work in some incredibly dry, hot areas where even plants look parched.) Suddenly he calls the well digger and indicates where digging should begin. Food and thanks are offered as the seeker indicates at how great a depth the water is. I have never known a water diviner to get it wrong yet; their understanding is truly astonishing. The well digger himself knows which earth spirits he is likely to encounter and at what depths, and before digging commences a special oracle is produced or pebbles thrown to indicate which offerings should be made to placate the spirits down below. To dig without doing this would be extremely dangerous and could result in the sudden death of the digger. Wells have been known to collapse on top of well diggers, while others have suddenly died for no obvious reason at all. In view of this, all precautions are taken. I once asked a well digger if he had ever seen any earth spirits while digging and he proceeded to describe the small brown or grey entities that emerge from the soil at certain depths. 'They are small, with large teeth and many eyes,' he told me. They can surround the digger in panic and if the correct offerings have not been made he can be choked by their breath, 'which steals the soul'. To die in the earth under these circumstances is extremely bad luck and a human soul can be lost and *never* be reborn.

Respecting the Earth

The earth is magic, bizarre and beautiful. It is our past and future, and holds the keys to our survival. The greatest wisdom of the earth is respect. It offers us the hope that we will be reunited with the universe at some point, though we will always form some essential component of the earth. We are of it, formed in the antiquity of time and so we will remain.

By setting up shrines and honouring the earth, the traditional religions of Africa ensure that respect is never lost. Sadly in the Western world too many people have lost touch with the earth. There is too much emphasis on the material things that surround us, and people in developed countries are moving further and further away from the notion of a 'spiritual, living earth'. The concept of the earth being both spiritual and physical may be a hard one to grasp, and it is a notion that can only truly be understood after much thought.

To traditional peoples like the Balanta, Manjack, Senufo or Papel, the interdependent universe is an everyday reality. Our universe is linked by spiritual power, threads that may remain unseen to ordinary people but which are real none the less. There is a deep acceptance that we are thus joined to time and space. Our earth is not merely the rock covered in plants and other life that science espouses. Instead it is a spiritual entity in it own right. It can be contacted and *is* contacted.

In the village of Kouniara, where Aliou and I grew up, there is a place where 'the earth breathes'. It is a sacred spot surrounded by dense forest that has an aura of magic attached to it. The spirit of the place seems to hang from the leaves and branches of the trees. At noon, when cicadas normally sing, this place is quiet. It has a stillness and a powerful beauty, yet it is feared since people have died mysteriously after inhaling the air. Some years ago the village elders decided to ask the spirits what they wanted. Why did they kill people at this place? It was also thought that they might be able to help the village in some way. They carried out a special divination ceremony in that most sacred forest. All manner of offerings were made and a startling answer was received. A strange spirit of green and yellow light appeared to one of the elders that same night. It identified itself as the guardian of the earth at that place, and it offered to help and advise the village *for a price*. One elder would have to agree to make an offering at the site of a pure white bull. *However*, the man making the offering would die within two days of doing so. If this was carried out then the village would prosper; if not it would stagnate. Consultations were held among the village elders but none of them wanted to make the sacrifice, since they would also become part of it. The debate has continued for many years and the village has seen its fortunes decline.

This story illustrates the power of the earth and the demands it will make if it is not satisfied with human reasons for consulting it. It is said that the elders of the village should have consulted the earth spirit without thinking of what it could do for them. That was the mistake. An alliance should have been made and the earth spirit would probably have offered to help in its own time. In exchange for human dishonesty in contacting it, a high price has been demanded and this will not be easy to satisfy, though if the decline of the village is to be halted, it may have to be.

Earth wisdom is everywhere. It is available to us if we choose to accept it. It is found through direct contacts which may follow our offerings and tokens of respect. Earth wisdom is found in the energies that criss-cross our planet, and is embodied in sacred stones, streams and mountains. It may also appear to us in dreams. It is powerful and must be respected at all times, though at the same time it can be a friend to humanity. Learning to respect the earth and therefore to understand it is the greatest kindness that we can afford it.

FURTHER READING

Akpabo, Ekepe S., *Ibibio Music in Nigerian Culture*, Michigan State University Press, 1975

Atkins, Guy, *Manding, Focus on an African Civilisation*, School of Oriental & African Studies (London)

Chesi, Gert, *The Last Africans*, Worgl, Austria: Perlinger, 1977

Chidester, David, *Religions of South Africa*, Routledge (London and New York), 1992

Dettwyler, Katherine A., *Dancing Skeletons: Life and death in West Africa*, Waveland Press, 1994

Dieterlen, Germaine, *Essai sur la religion Bambara*, Paris, 1951

Dieterlen, Germaine, *Les Ames des Dogons*, Paris, 1941

Dieterlen, Germaine & Griaule, M., *The Pale Fox*, Paris Institute of Ethnography, 1965

Fernandez, J.W., *Bwiti, an ethnography of the religious imagination in Africa*, Princeton University Press, 1982

Gibbal, Jean Marie, *Genii of the River Niger*, University of Chicago Press, 1994

Graham, Alistair & Beard, Peter, *Eyelids Of Morning: The Mingled Destinies Of Crocodiles and Men*, Chronicle Books (San Francisco), 1990

Grenville, Robert Kyle, *The Sirius Mystery*, Sidgwick & Jackson, 1976

Griaule, Marcel, *Conversations with Ogotemmeli*, Oxford University Press, 1965

Handem, Diana Lima, *Nature et fonctionnment du pouvoir chez les Balanta Brassa*, Lisboa, 1985

Henry, Christine, *Les iles ou dansent les enfants defunts: age, sexe et pouvoir chez les Bijogo de Guine Bissau*, Paris (CNRS), 1994

Henry, Jos, *L'ame d'un people Africaine, Les Bambara: leur vie psychique, ethique, sociale, religieuse*, Munster, Aschendorff, 1910

Imperato, Pascal James, *African Folk Medicine: practices and beliefs of the Bambara and other peoples*, York Press (Baltimore), 1977

Linares, Olga F., *Power, Prayer and Production: The Jola of Casamance, Senegal*, Cambridge University Press, 1992

Mark, Peter, *A cultural, economic and religious history of the Basse Casamance since 1500*, F. Steiner (Stuttgart), 1985

Paterson, Jacqueline Memory, *Tree Wisdom*, Thorsons, 1996

Pritchard, E.E. Evans (Sir), *Man and Woman among the Azande*, London, 1974

Pritchard, E.E. Evans (Sir), *Witchcraft, Oracles and Magic among the Azande*, 1937 (Republished in 1976 by Clarendon Press)

Ross, Doran H., *Elephant: The animal and its ivory in African culture*, University of Los Angeles (UCLA), 1992

Sagnia, B.K., *A concise account of the history and traditions of origin of major Gambian ethnic groups*, The Gambia National Museum

Société de Saint Augustin, *Chez Les Fangs, ou quinze années de sejour au Congo français*, Lille, 1912

Swiderski, Stanislaw, *Histoire de la religion Bouiti*, Saarbrucken, 1978

Talbot, Dorothy Amaury, *Life In Southern Nigeria*, Macmillan & Co., 1923

Talbot, Dorothy Amaury, *Women's Mysteries of a Primitive People: The Ibibios of Southern Nigeria*, Cassell & Co., 1915

Tauxier, Louis, *Histoire des Bambaras*, Paris, 1942

Tauxier, Louis, *La Religion Bambara*, Paris, 1927

Torday, E., *Camp and Tramp in African Wilds*, Seeley, Service & Co.
  Ltd, 1913

Zahan, D. & Solange de Ganay, *Études sur la cosmologie des dogons et des Bambaras du Soudan français*, London, 1951

USEFUL ADDRESSES

The Museum Of Mankind (The British Museum's Ethnography
   Department)
6 Burlington Gardens
London W1X 2EX
020 7323 8044

The Royal Anthropological Institute
50 Fitzroy Street
London W1P 5HS
020 7387 0455

Goldsmiths College
Lewisham Way
New Cross
London SE14 6NW
020 7919 7171

School for Oriental and African Studies
University of London
Thornhaugh Street
Russell Square
London WC1H 0XG
020 7637 2388
www.soas.ac.uk

The African Books Collective Ltd
27 The Jam Factory
Park End Street
Oxford OX1 1HU
01865 726686

The African Association
109 St James Road
Northampton NN5 5LD
01604 758999

The African Community Involvement Association
224 Eagle House
London Road
Mitcham
Surrey CR4 3HD
020 8687 2400

The Embassy of the Republic of Senegal
39 Marloes Road
London W8 6LA
020 7938 4048

INDEX

Piatkus Books

If you have enjoyed reading this book, you may be interested in other titles published by Piatkus. These include:

The Afterlife: An investigation into the mysteries of life after death Jenny Randles and Peter Hough

Ambika's Guide To Healing And Wholeness: The energetic path to the chakras and colour Ambika Wauters

Art Of Sexual Magic, The: How to use sexual energy to transform your life Margot Anand

As I See It: A psychic's guide to developing your healing and sensing abilities Betty F. Balcombe

Ask Your Angels: A practical guide to working with angels to enrich your life Alma Daniel, Timothy Wyllie and Andrew Ramer

At Peace In The Light: A man who died twice reveals amazing insights into life, death and its mysteries Dannion Brinkley with Paul Perry

Barefoot Doctor's Handbook for Heroes: A spiritual guide to fame and fortune Barefoot Doctor

Barefoot Doctor's Handbook for Modern Lovers: A spiritual guide to truly rude and amazing love and sex Barefoot Doctor

Barefoot Doctor's Handbook for the Urban Warrior: A spiritual survival guide Barefoot Doctor

Beyond Belief: How to develop mystical consciousness and discover the God within Peter Spink

Book of Shadows: A modern Witch reveals the wisdom of Witchcraft and the power of the Goddess Phyllis Currott

Care Of The Soul: How to add depth and meaning to your everyday life Thomas Moore

Changes: A guide to personal transformation and new ways of living in the new millennium Soozi Holbeche

Channelling For Everyone: A safe, step-by-step guide to developing your intuition and psychic abilities Tony Neate

Channelling: What it is and how to do it Lita de Alberdi

Child Of Eternity, A: An extraordinary young girl's message from the world beyond Adriana Rocha and Kristi Jorde

Piatkus Books

For the Very Best in Mind, Body and Spirit

African Wisdom is part of Piatkus Books' new Mind, Body and Spirit series. Each of these accessible and inspiring introductions is written by an expert in the field. Titles include: **Meditation, Celtic Wisdom, Tarot, The Essential Nostradamus, Feng Shui, Crystal Wisdom, Reiki, Psychic Awareness, Colour Healing, Angels, Shamanism, Astrology, Earth Mysteries, Druidry** and **Kabbalah.** Forthcoming titles include: **Pendulum Dowsing, Atlantis, Native American Wisdom, Macrobiotics, Radionics, Auras, Chakras** and **Palmistry.**

These beautifully designed, in-depth introductions cost only £5.99. For a free brochure with our complete list of titles, please write to:

Piatkus Books
5 Windmill Street
London W1P 1HF

Tel: 0171 631 0710

Email: info@piatkus.co.uk
Website: www.piatkus.co.uk